HISTORIC
COMMUNITIES

Tools and Gadgets

Bobbie Kalman

Crabtree Publishing Company

www.crabtreebooks.com

Toronto·Oxford·New York

HISTORIC
COMMUNITIES

Created by Bobbie Kalman

For Diane and Bernie
Bajardi

Illustrations
Antoinette "Cookie" Debiasi

Research and editing
Jodi Gaspich

Design and mechanicals
Antoinette "Cookie" Debiasi

Color Seperations
ISCOA
Systems Color

Printer
Worzalla Publishing Company

Crabtree Publishing Company
www.crabtreebooks.com   1-800-387-7650

Cataloguing in Publication Data
Kalman, Bobbie, 1947-
   Tools and gadgets

(Historic communities series)
Includes index.
ISBN 0-86505-488-6 (library bound) ISBN 0-86505-508-4 (pbk.)

1. Tools - History - Juvenile literature. 2. Implements, utensils, etc. -
History - Juvenile - literature. 3. Frontier and pioneer life - Juvenile
literature. I. Title. II. Series: Kalman, Bobbie, 1947 -
Historic communities.

TJ1195.K35 1992   j680'.9   LC93-6217

**Published in
the United States**
PMB 16A
350 Fifth Ave.
Suite 3308
New York, NY
10118

**Published
in Canada**
616 Welland Ave.,
St. Catharines,
Ontario, Canada
L2M 5V6

**Published in the
United Kingdom**
73 Lime Walk
Headington
Oxford
OX3 7AD
United Kingdom

**Published
in Australia**
386 Mt. Alexander Rd.,
Ascot Vale (Melbourne)
V1C 3032

Contents

All the tools and gadgets on these shelves were made from natural materials. Most of them have been carved from wood. They are works of art that have lasted well over one hundred years!

Useful objects from another time

Have you ever visited an historic home, village, or town? Do you remember listening to guides who explained the uses of objects from the past? Those objects were likely tools and gadgets that were made more than one hundred years ago.

This cherry pitter pits cherries in split seconds. Say it five times!

What are tools and gadgets?

A tool is anything that assists a person in getting work done. Hammers, saws, drills, and screwdrivers are the objects we commonly call tools. In the old days a tool was described as the extension of the human hand. In later days some tools and gadgets were powered by animals, wind, and water. Most of today's tools are operated by electricity or batteries.

A gadget is a clever device that performs a small job. A gadget is a tool, too. The jobs that gadgets perform, however, can also be accomplished using ordinary tools. The cherry pitter shown on this page, for example, pits cherries, but cherries can also be pitted with a knife, which is a more common tool.

The dog in the wheel must do a lot of running to churn a little butter!

Natural materials

The tools and gadgets of the past were made from natural materials such as wood, leather, bone, and metals such as iron and steel. Today's tools and gadgets are made from plastic, rubber, and other synthetic materials. They may save time and energy, but they cannot match the beauty of the handmade tools of the past, which were carefully designed and made by the artisans who used them.

Many of these traditional tools are still used today.

What is inside the barrel and jar?
If it gets out, will it go far?

The gadget above made life sweeter.
The one to the right performed like
clockwork. The snippy thing below
could put your lights out. Can you
guess what these gadgets are?

Mystery tools and gadgets

Look at the pictures on this page and guess how the tools and gadgets shown were used in the past. If you look carefully, you will see the uses of most of these objects throughout the book. If the clues have left you stumped, you can find out what these objects are and how they work on page 31—but do not look up the answers yet! After you have read the book, you will figure out the answers for yourself. Happy hunting!

Here are some clues to help you identify the gadgets on this page: 1. Squeeze out air—make fire flare! 2. This magic box is lots of fun. Do you know how it is run? 3. A giant pitcher hangs in space. It tells about a drinking place. What is it? 4. This nasty tool might make you drool and scream and yell like a silly fool! 5. Butter's done; dog's gone.

This bedroom from the past may look comfortable, but it was very cold in the winter. How many "warming" gadgets can you find in this book?

This old washing machine has a wringer for squeezing water from wet clothes.

Home gadgets

There was no gas, electricity, or running water in the homes of the past. People had to bring in water from a well, wash dishes and clothes by hand, and make the candles that provided light for reading and other nighttime activities.

The gadgets shown on these pages helped the settlers stay warm and keep their clothes looking clean and neat. Which modern gadgets or appliances have taken the place of each of these objects? Which objects are no longer used?

In the early days, tinder boxes were used to start fires because there were no matches. **Tinder** *is material that catches fire easily. Shreds of linen rags made up the tinder. When steel was rubbed against flint, a hard, bumpy mineral, the sparks created from the friction set the tinder on fire. The tinder box was often the bottom part of a candlestick.*

Candles were made by pouring melted animal fat, called **tallow**, into a mold such as this one.

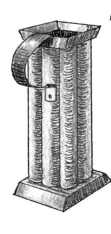

Burning coals were put inside this iron to make it hot enough to smooth out wrinkles.

Shoe scrapers could be found outside many doors. Since animals roamed freely in the old days, the settlers had many unwanted things stuck to the bottoms of their shoes.

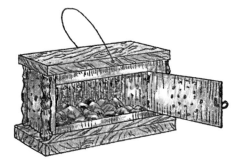

Foot warmers were filled with hot coals that radiated heat. They kept settler toes toasty warm.

In winter the wind rattled the windows and blew fiercely down the chimneys. Going to bed was a chilling experience, but the settlers made it a little more bearable by warming their beds with a warming pan. They filled the pan with hot coals and moved it quickly around between the covers so the sheets would not get scorched.

washing stick

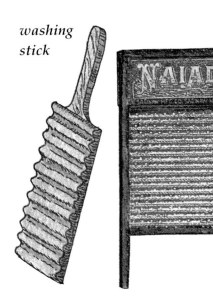

wash board

The early settlers washed their clothes using a homemade wooden washing stick. In later days they were able to buy wash boards, which were much wider. Some may have even had washing machines such as the one shown on the opposite page.

Tools, gadgets, and utensils surround the settler fireplace. A crane swings in and out supporting pots and kettles. It allowed the cook of the past to stir food away from the flames of the fire. A clock jack hangs from the mantle. Its purpose was to turn a roast of meat so that its sides would brown evenly. It was wound like a clock. Another type of clock jack can be seen on page 6. It is a clockwork spit jack. It was used to turn a roast on a spit. On the right side of the fireplace is a spittoon for tobacco chewers. The bellows was for fanning the fire, and the old birch broom kept the floor clean.

Food gadgets

The kitchens of the past had no refrigerators, running water, electric stoves, or microwave ovens, but the settlers had plenty of gadgets to help them prepare and cook their food. The kitchen fireplace provided the fire for cooking. Grain was crushed into flour using a **mortar** and **pestle**. Cream was dashed to make fresh butter in a **butter churn**. Apples were cored and peeled with an apple peeler, and nutmeg and peppercorns were ground in a spice mill. Sugar was sold in cones. A sugar cutter was needed to break pieces from it.

Long-handled frying pans that sat on three legs were called **spiders.**

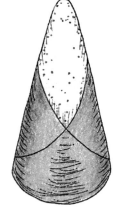

Apple cider was made by crushing apples in an apple press.

In the early days sugar was sold in cones. Sugar cutters were used to snip off small pieces. Did you identify the one on page 6?

A mortar (bowl) and pestle (stick) were used to crush grain into flour. ⟶

Butter was made by pumping cream up and down in a wooden butter churn. Sometimes dogs carried out this tiresome chore. (See pages 5 and 7 for pictures of dog churns.)

The apple peeler was a gadget that peeled and cored apples. It could remove the peel in one piece!

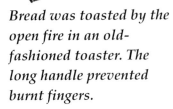

Bread was toasted by the open fire in an old-fashioned toaster. The long handle prevented burnt fingers.

Spices such as nutmeg were ground in a spice mill.

11

One never knew what treasures could be found on the shelves of the general store. The customer in the picture above would like to have a look at some silver cutlery that was imported from England. The picture on the left shows tools that were made in the community. The blackboard displays the prices of some locally grown produce.

In the general store

The general store was full of wonderful tools and gadgets for use and for sale. Its shelves were lined with exotic spices, mouth-watering candies, and mysterious objects. The farmers and craftspeople from the community traded their produce and crafts at the general store for local goods and for products from faraway places.

Fans were the air conditioners of the past. They were made of ivory, feathers, bone, silk, or paper.

The food that was to be sold at the general store was stored in containers such as sacks and barrels. Sugar cones were wrapped in paper. All these containers could be called "storage tools."

Would you want to get your mustache wet if you were drinking tea? This mustache cup guarantees to keep it dry.

This gadget, called a **goffer,** *ironed the bows and frills on bonnets and collars.*

Whale-oil lamps produced very little smoke. They gave off a bright light because each lamp had two wicks. The pin was turned to raise the wick when its end burned down.

The settler barn was filled with tools that were used for planting and harvesting crops as well as gadgets that helped farmers prepare the foods they harvested.

At the farm

Most of the people in the old days were farmers. Do you know why? Today we can go to the supermarket and buy any kind of food we want. In the early days almost every family grew its own food and raised livestock as a source of milk and meat.

*A **winnower** was used to separate the thin outer cover from the wheat kernel. A farmer scooped up grains with a winnower and threw them into the air, allowing the unwanted shells to be blown away.*

Using simple tools and animal power, the farmers of the past prepared the land and planted and harvested their crops. Many had to make their own tools, too. The tools on this page are typical of the ones that would have been found in the barns of more than one hundred years ago. They were used by the farmers of those early times.

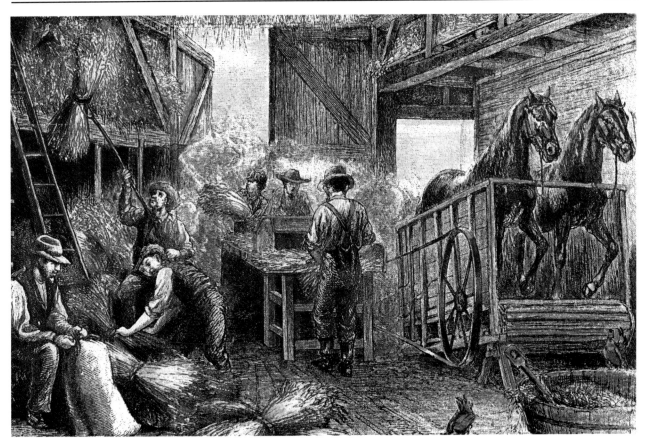

This **threshing machine,** *powered by horses on a treadmill, shakes the seeds from stalks of wheat and deposits them in a bin outside the barn. The leftover straw is used to feed animals.*

Pokes *were wooden braces placed around the necks of animals to stop them from getting through fences.*

Long *stalks of grain were harvested with a* **cradle.** *A cradle is a* **scythe** *with three fingers and a blade.*

A wooden hay fork was used to gather straw and hay.

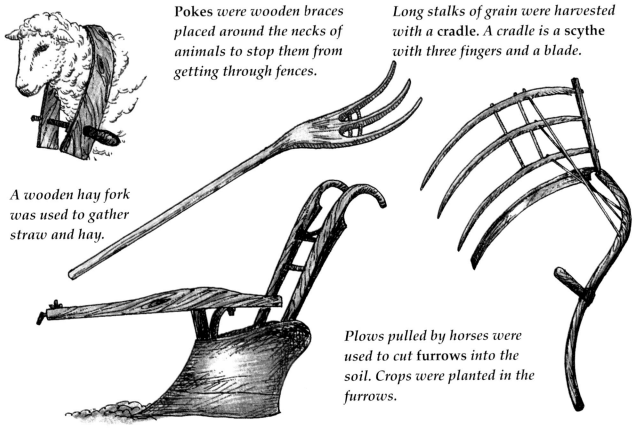

Plows pulled by horses were used to cut **furrows** *into the soil. Crops were planted in the furrows.*

A waterwheel

The waterwheel of a mill (shown in the top drawing) turned as water flowed over it. The gears inside the mill (above) transferred the power of the water to the top millstone, which ground the grain as it turned.

A millstone

The mill pick was used to cut grooves, called **furrows**, into the millstones. These grooves ripped and ground the grain. What is another kind of furrow?

Mills were giant tools

The gristmill and sawmill are two examples of mills that performed difficult jobs for the settlers. Each of these mills could be considered a huge tool that accomplished one main job. The gristmill ground grain into flour, and the sawmill cut logs into planks.

Clockwise from top left: The **muley saw** *cut logs into planks quickly and easily. The saw was powered by a waterwheel under the mill. The sawyer stacks the finished lumber behind the sawmill.*

Grinding grain by hand into enough flour to make a loaf of bread could take several hours. Cutting logs into planks was also very difficult when it was done by hand. People saved time and energy when they used mills, instead of muscles, to accomplish these tasks.

Before there were sawmills, people had to cut planks the hard way, using a **pit saw** *such as the one on the right.*

A pit saw

*The **forge** was the most important "tool" of many metalworkers. Without fire, metal could not be heated and pounded into shape. The forge was made of brick.*

A tub of water stood near the forge to cool down the iron and the blacksmith's tongs.

Tools used by the blacksmith

Metalworking tools

There were many types of metalworkers in the early days. The founder, farrier, silversmith, tinsmith, and cutler are just a few examples. Some metalworkers created objects by pounding and bending them into shape. These were known as the **smiths** because they hit or "smite" hot metal. Using molds, other metalworkers cast metals into shape. Some metalworkers, such as the silversmith, did both.

The most common metalworker was the blacksmith. Each household, farm, and workshop required his services. The blacksmith made locks, fireplace utensils, nails, horseshoes, hoops for barrels, and metal tires for wheels. He heated iron, hammered it, cut it, and sometimes joined it with steel.

The founder

The founder heated different metals together to make new metals in a process called **smelting**. Through smelting, copper and zinc became brass, and copper and tin became bronze. The metals were melted in a heat-resistant pot called a **crucible**. The crucible was laid in the hot coals of the forge. The bellows were used to make the coals hotter.

The founder poured hot metal into molds to make objects such as candlesticks.

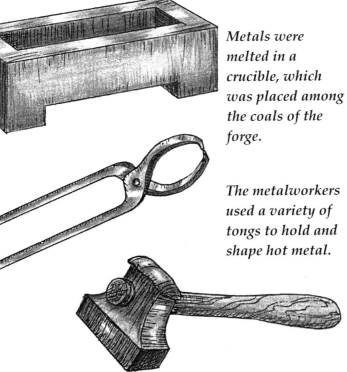

Metals were melted in a crucible, which was placed among the coals of the forge.

The metalworkers used a variety of tongs to hold and shape hot metal.

This hammer, called a set hammer or flatter, was used by metalworkers for smoothing out the surface of metal.

The bellows brought air to the fire to make the coals hotter. When the blacksmith pulled the chain, the bellows squeezed together, forcing the air inside to blow into the forge. When he let the chain go, the bellows filled with air again. Did you identify the bellows on page 7?

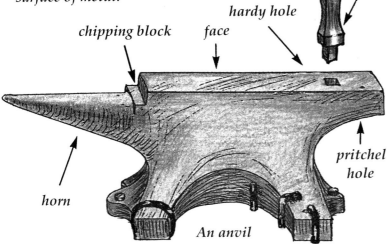

chipping block   face   hardy hole   hardy

horn

pritchel hole

An anvil

Objects made by the founder

The cabinetmaker made fine furniture. He aged the wood out-doors until it was strong enough to use. The wood was then turned, carved, and joined together to make cabinets, tables, chairs, and beds.

*A **plane** was used for shaving wood to make it smooth.*

Woodworking tools

In the old days wood was the most plentiful raw material available to the settlers. Trees were everywhere, and various types of wood were available. As a result many craftspeople learned the art of working with wood. They made all kinds of useful objects. Cabinetmakers made furniture, coopers made barrels, wheelwrights made wheels, and carpenters built houses. Woodworkers had to know the strengths and weaknesses of each type of wood so they could use the most suitable ones for the objects they were creating.

Even though they created different kinds of objects, woodworkers used many of the same tools. Lathes, planes, drawknives, axes, adzes, and shavinghorses could be seen in most woodworking workshops.

The cooper used a **drawknife** to carve curves into barrel **staves**.

A shavinghorse

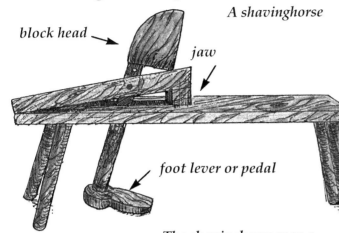

block head

jaw

foot lever or pedal

The shavinghorse was a carpenter bench that allowed woodworkers to sit as they shaped a piece of wood. The pedal locked the wood securely under the jaw of the bench and released it when the piece was finished.

The **lathe** was the main power tool of many woodworkers. It was operated by turning a large wheel. The lathe spun a piece of wood horizontally and allowed the woodworker to shape it with special chisels.

The broadax was strong enough to cut through hardwood logs. It was used for chopping.

The **adze** was used for making round logs square by chipping away bits of wood. The squared logs were then cut using a pit saw. The adze was also useful for hollowing out logs.

The long, sharp point of the **auger** bored holes into wood.

The drawknife could be found in every woodworking shop. It was used to shave thin layers from wood until the wood was the right shape. Some drawknives had curved blades.

The printing shop

In a small community the printer printed the village newspaper, advertisements, and announcements. Some larger printing shops also printed books.

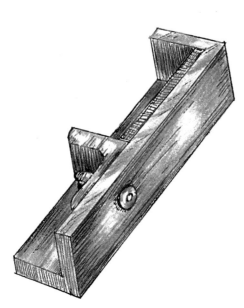

Words and sentences were typeset on a composing stick.

The letters are inked with a brayer.

The paper is pressed against the inked characters when the handle of the press is pulled.

Setting the type

Today, newspapers are typeset on a computer. To typeset words in the early days, the printer first placed the letters, one by one, onto a **composing stick**. The type, which was backwards, was arranged from right to left, so that it would be read left to right when it was printed. Small pieces of lead were placed between the words, lines, and pictures to create the white spaces. These white spaces are called **leading**.

Preparing the galley

When the stick was full, the printer transferred the type to a shallow wooden tray called a **galley**, tied it, and slid the assembled page onto the **imposing stone**. The type was then locked in a rectangular frame called a **chase** and moved to the printing press.

The ink was spread onto the type with a roller, called a **brayer**. The printer then pressed the paper firmly against the type by pulling the press handle. Two to three hundred pages could be **pressed**, or printed, in one hour!

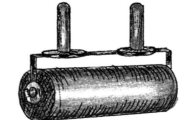

A brayer

The printer stands at the composing table typesetting an advertisement. Notice that the letters and picture are set opposite to how they will be read.

The type is transferred from the composing stick to the galley.

*The type was a small block of metal with a letter, or **character**, at one end.*

*The printer kept his type in four **type cases** full of cubby holes or compartments. Each compartment contained different letters. The capital letters were in the upper two cases, and the small letters in the lower two cases. For this reason capital letters are sometimes called "upper-case" letters and regular letters are known as "lower-case."*

Doctors had tools for amputation, bloodletting, cupping, dentistry, and instruments used for delivering babies.

Medical gadgets

The doctors of the past knew very little about what made people sick. As a result many people, especially young children, died of diseases that could easily be cured today.

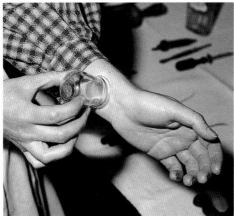

Cups were heated and placed on the skin to form blisters. It was believed that diseases could be drawn out of the body and into the blisters.

Leeches were bloodletting tools.

Doctors examined patients to try to find out why they were sick. They prescribed treatments to make them well. If someone broke an arm or a leg, doctors set the broken bones by putting leather or wooden splints around the fracture, somewhat like a cast. If the bone did not heal, the limb was cut off!

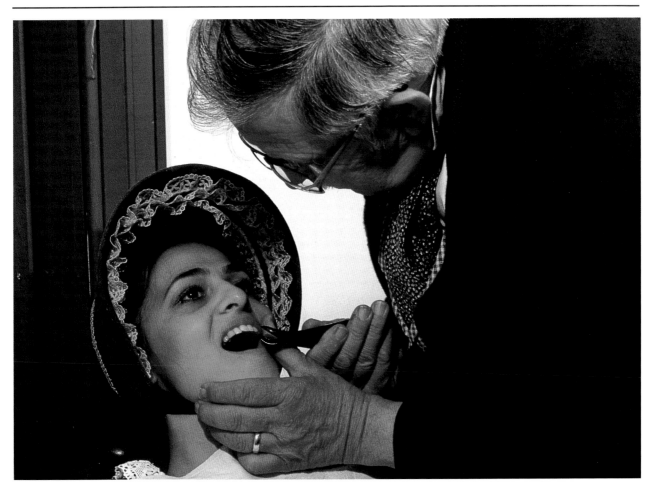

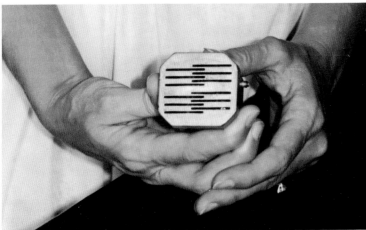

Doctors also acted as dentists. When a tooth was diseased, there was only one thing to do—pull it out. In later days dentists discovered that teeth could be drilled and filled. Did you guess that one of the mystery objects on page 7 was an old dentist drill?

The settlers believed that many diseases could be cured by ridding the body of harmful fluids. Bloodletting was a popular treatment for all kinds of ailments. Blood was let by making incisions either with a **scarificator**, shown above, or a **fleam**, illustrated at right. Neither of these gadgets, however, was as natural as a leech when it came to bloodletting, or bloodsucking, as the case may be.

A fleam used for bloodletting

Children's toys and gadgets

Both the Noah's Ark, above, and Jacob's Ladder, in the photograph below, are children's toys that were inspired by the Bible. Jacob's Ladder is a chain of wooden blocks taped together in such a way that it looks as if the blocks are falling like a rope ladder falls from above. In a dream the prophet Jacob saw such a ladder reach from heaven to earth on which angels traveled back and forth.

The children of the settlers did not have many toys. They used their imaginations and made their own fun with a few simple items. For example, an old barrel hoop or an abandoned wagon-wheel tire could provide hours of enjoyment. Children chased these hoops over the vast, open countryside. They rolled the hoop, ran beside it, and kept it going by pushing it with a stick.

Although most of the settler children's toys were simple, there were a few fascinating gadgets such as magic lanterns, whirligigs, and stereoscopes that thrilled the children of long ago.

One could always find an old hoop for a fast game of hoop rolling.

A whirligig was a length of string strung through the hole of a round piece of wood. Pulling the string tight by the handles at either end and then relaxing it made the wooden disk spin quickly and move from one end of the string to the other.

The magic lantern was an old-time slide projector. Inside the box was an oil lamp and a reflector that focused light onto a painted glass slide. The picture on the slide was projected onto a wall. Magic-lantern shows fascinated children and adults!

A stereoscope thrilled children. When they looked through the viewer, they saw one three-dimensional image instead of the two identical ones on the cards.

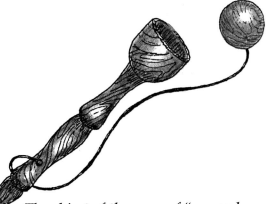

The object of the game of "cup and ball" was to swing the ball that was attached to the piece of string upwards and catch it with the cup.

27

Cards, hackles, wheels, and shuttles

The settlers could not buy their clothes in shops the way we do. Not only did they have to sew their own clothes, they also had to make the cloth from which the clothes were stitched. In the northern areas two kinds of raw materials were available from which cloth could be made: wool and flax. Sheep's wool became cozy winter clothing, and flax was spun into a lighter thread, called **line**, which was woven into **linen**. Those who lived in the south or near a town could also buy cotton fabric. Cotton was much thinner and more suitable for hot, summer weather. Below and opposite are the tools and gadgets used for making wool and linen.

This wool winder is called a **clock wheel.** *The thread wound around the wheel as it turned. A clock counted the number of strands in a skein of thread. At forty knots the spinner stopped to tie the knot.*

A loom

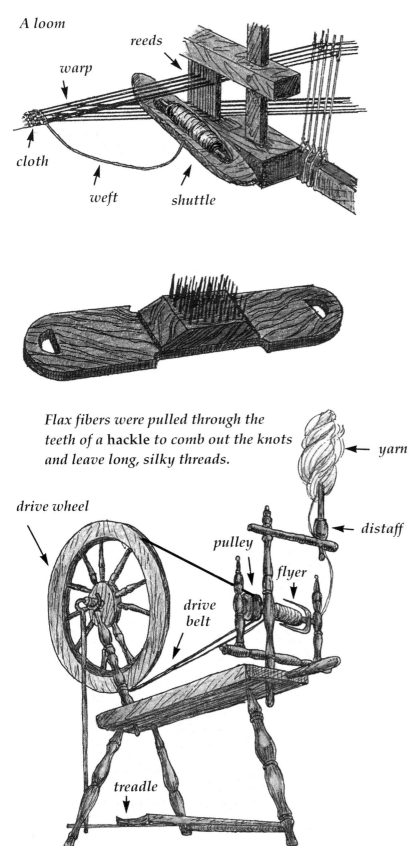

reeds

warp

cloth

weft

shuttle

A loom was used for weaving both wool and linen.

*Flax fibers were pulled through the teeth of a **hackle** to comb out the knots and leave long, silky threads.*

yarn

distaff

drive wheel

pulley

flyer

drive belt

treadle

A spinning wheel

Spinning is the act of making thread from wool or flax. The fibers are turned quickly, resulting in a long continuous thread.

Wool is untangled and fluffed with carding paddles before it is spun into yarn.

Yesterday and today

All the tools and gadgets shown below were used in the past. Name the objects or appliances that have replaced them. How are today's gadgets different from the ones pictured here?

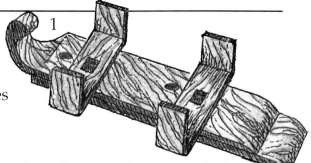

1

*A **ruggle** stopped a wagon wheel from rolling. What stops your bicycle or parent's car?*

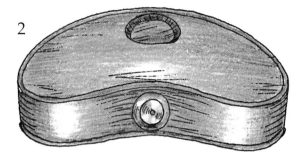

2

This gadget was known as a belly warmer. The houses of the past were very cold, so people had all kinds of gadgets to keep them warm. What other heating gadgets have you seen in this book? How do you stay warm?

3

Buckets such as these were kept filled with water to put out sudden fires. How are small household fires extinguished today?

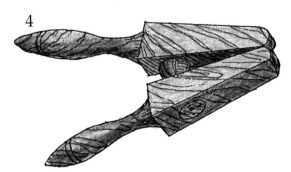

4

This is an old lemon squeezer. Do you have a modern one at home? How is it different from this one?

7

5

Milk was once kept in large cans. How is milk packaged today?

6

*People used to chop their vegetables with a **mezzaluna**, which means "half moon" in Italian. This curved knife was more commonly known as a cabbage chopper. Which appliances chop vegetables today?*

A rug beater was used to beat the dust from a carpet. How do you clean your carpets?

Glossary

amputation The process of cutting off a limb or part of a limb

appliance An electrical device such as a refrigerator or vacuum cleaner

chisel A metal cutting tool with a sharp angled edge

community 1. A group of people living in the same area and sharing goods, services, and a way of life. 2. The area in which they live

craftspeople People skilled in creating handmade goods

cutler A craftsperson who makes and repairs knives and other cutting instruments

device Any tool or gadget made for a special purpose

farrier A metalworker who specializes in making horseshoes and shoeing animals

flax A plant that yields a fine, light-colored fiber that is used to make linen

flint A hard mineral that makes a spark when it is struck with steel

friction The result of rubbing one object or surface against another

furrow 1. A shallow canal in the soil that has been cut with a plow and in which crops are planted. 2. A groove on a millstone that helps rip and grind grain

historic village A village from long ago that was preserved as an important part of the past

livestock Farm animals raised for food or to be sold for profit

lumber Any boards or planks that have been sawed from large pieces of wood

natural material Any material found in nature

produce Farm products such as fruits and vegetables

raw material Anything that is not manufactured or refined

sawyer A person who saws logs into planks

skein A length of yarn wound in a loose coil

spittoon A bowl-shaped vessel for spitting

stave A narrow strip of wood used to form the side of a barrel

synthetic material An artificial material that was made by people

tallow Melted and cleaned animal fat that was used for making soap and candles

threshing The act of beating wheat and other grains to remove their kernels

tinder Any material, such as shredded rags, that readily catches fire

tinsmith A craftsperson who works with tin

treadmill A mechanism operated by walking on a belt that turns on wheels

type A small block of metal with a raised character that is used in printing

utensil Any instrument or container used in the kitchen to aid in a chore

Answers

Page 6: (top) Leeches were transported in small barrels and stored in pots or jars. See drawing of leech on page 24; (middle) Sugar cutters—see page 11; (right) The clockwork spit jack turned meat on a spit. The works were wound like a clock, and with each "tick" the roast turned; (bottom) Candle snuffer.
Page 7: 1. The air from the bellows made a fire hotter. (See page 19.) 2. A magic lantern (See page 27.) 3. The pitcher is a sign advertising a tavern. Not many people knew how to read, so the signs above shops and taverns showed pictures of what was inside. 4. An early dentist drill was operated by pumping the foot pedal up and down. 5. This butter churn churned butter when a dog ran inside the wheel. (See page 5.)
Answers to page 30:
1. Brakes 2. See page 9 for heating gadgets. 3. Fire extinguishers 4. Today's lemon squeezers are usually round. 5. Milk comes in cartons, jugs, and bags. 6. Food processors 7. Today's carpets are cleaned with vacuum cleaners.

Index

Acknowledgments

Illustrations and cover design: Antoinette DeBiasi
Cover art: John Mantha
Photographs:
Marc Crabtree (at Black Creek Pioneer Village): cover, pages 4, 6 (bottom left), 7 (bottom), 12 (top), 16 (right), 23 (top), 24 (top), 29 (middle and bottom)
Peter Crabtree and Bobbie Kalman: (At Genesee Country Village), pages 26, 27 (top); (At Colonial Williamsburg) pages 6 (top left and right), 7 (top, middle center), 19 (top), 25 (bottom); (At other historic sites) pages 7 (middle left), 8 (bottom)

Black Creek Pioneer Village/TRCA: page 11 (all), 12 (bottom right), 22 (bottom), 25 (top)
Jim Bryant: pages 12 (bottom left), 18, 19 (bottom), 20, 24 (bottom)
Ken Faris: Title page, pages 17 (all three), 21 (top), 22 (top), 23 (bottom), 29 (top)
Todmorden Mills: page 8 (top)
Environment Canada: page 10
Bob Mansour: pages 7 (middle right), 21 (bottom)
Colonial Williamsburg Foundation: page 16 (left)

3 4 5 6 7 8 9 0 Printed in the USA 9 8 7 6 5 4

Inside Mary's fossil shop, visitors crowded around her latest discoveries. They came from all over Europe to meet her and ask her questions. After they left, Mary packaged up the fossils that collectors had bought. She built a wooden frame for each one, and then gently placed it inside and packed it with plaster.

Some of the fossils traveled by ship across the ocean to North America, and other fossils traveled by wagon to London and places that were closer.

Mary was used to finding creatures that looked as if they swam in the water. But the creature she found next, still tucked in the cliff, was completely different.

It was shorter than Mary and—could it be?—it appeared to have wings and a beak. It must have been an ancient bird or a bat.

The creature turned out to be a "winged lizard" or "pterosaur," the first one ever found in England. Mary closed her eyes and tried to imagine it flapping overhead.

Slowly, slowly, bone by bone, Mary's fossil finds were adding to the knowledge that scientists had about Earth and its history. Her discoveries helped change what scientists chose to study from then on.

Some scientists were becoming experts in new kinds of science, such as geology, the study of rocks. Other scientists were fascinated by paleontology, the study of fossils and ancient life.

Meanwhile, day after day, year after year, Mary walked by the sea. Bone by bone, fossil by fossil, she learned more and more.